BIOGRAPHY FROM
ANCIENT CIVILIZATIONS
LEGENDS, FOLKLORE, AND STORIES OF ANCIENT WORLDS

The Life and Times of

BUDDHA

Mitchell Lane
PUBLISHERS

P.O. Box 196
Hockessin, Delaware 19707

BIOGRAPHY FROM ANCIENT CIVILIZATIONS
LEGENDS, FOLKLORE, AND STORIES OF ANCIENT WORLDS

Titles in the Series

The Life and Times of:

BIOGRAPHY FROM
ANCIENT CIVILIZATIONS
LEGENDS, FOLKLORE, AND STORIES OF ANCIENT WORLDS

The Life and Times of

BUDDHA

Mona Gedney

Mitchell Lane
PUBLISHERS

Printing   1   2   3   4   5   6   7   8

Library of Congress Cataloging-in-Publication Data

Gedney, Mona K.
    The life and times of Buddha / by Mona Gedney.
        p. cm. — (Biography from ancient civilizations) (Life and times of)
    Includes bibliographical references and index.
    ISBN 1-58415-342-3 (library bound : alk. paper)
    1. Gautama Buddha—Juvenile literature. 2. Buddhists—India—Biography—Juvenile literature. I. Title. II. Series. III. Series: Life and times of
BQ892.G43 2005
294.3'63—dc22

                          2004024606

ABOUT THE AUTHOR: Mona Gedney has been a teacher for thirty-three years and has published sixteen books and numerous short stories. She has a deep-rooted interest in people and places, and her own reading includes essays, history, biography, and travel, as well as fiction, particularly mysteries. She lives in West Lafayette, Indiana.

PHOTO CREDITS: Cover, pp. 1, 3, 6, 9, 28, 41—Jamie Kondrchek; p. 10—Brahmins; p. 14—Metropolitan Museum of Art; p. 20—Golden Land Pages; p. 22—Love Those Gifts; p. 32—Dharma Art Gallery; pp. 34, 36—Asian Art; p. 38—Theravada.ca; p. 40—Thekchen Choling Gallery.

BIOGRAPHY FROM
ANCIENT CIVILIZATIONS
LEGENDS, FOLKLORE, AND STORIES OF ANCIENT WORLDS

The Life and Times of

BUDDHA

*For Your Information

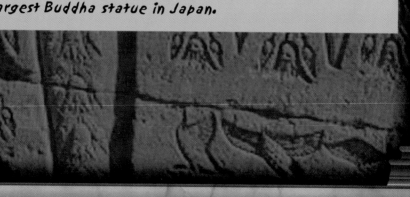

The Great Buddha of Kamakura, built in the 1200s, is a bronze statue that stands 13.35 meters tall and weighs 93 tons. Originally, it was inside a large hall, but the hall was washed away by a tsunami. It is the second largest Buddha statue in Japan.

CHAPTER ONE

THE BUDDHA

Hot sunlight beat down upon the dusty roadway, but no one seemed to notice it. In the grove at the edge of town, a crowd had gathered around a tall, regal man in a saffron robe. The people were listening carefully to his every word. Even the birds in the trees were silent as he spoke. Although he did not raise his voice or speak with intense emotion, he held the complete attention of his audience. He was a Buddha.

Suddenly the crowd separated, allowing a young woman carrying a baby to approach the speaker. Some people were annoyed by the interruption. They changed their minds when they looked at her. Tears rolled down her face as she looked from the son she cradled in her arms to the face of the Buddha.

"Please, Lord," she begged. "Give my son a medicine that will restore him."

The Buddha stopped speaking as she drew close. He looked at her compassionately. He could see at a glance that the infant in her arms was dead, but he did not say so.

"You must go from house to house," he told her. "Each time you find one that death has not touched, beg of the people there a mustard seed. Once you have done so, bring the seeds back to me."

Grateful to be offered even a glimmer of hope, she nodded eagerly and then hurried to the closest house to begin her search. As she went from door to door, however, she found the same answer. She could not collect any mustard seeds. Death had touched each household. No family had been spared.

After knocking on many doors, she realized why the Buddha had given her such a task. Death could not be escaped and it spared no family. That knowledge saddened her. It also helped her to bear the loss of her son. Slowly she returned to tell him that she understood and to thank him for his kindness. Later still, she would become one of his followers.

"So it is with all of life," the Buddha told the crowd as she departed once more, this time to prepare her son's funeral. "All things are fleeting. Nothing lasts."

He pointed to a nearby champaka tree whose golden blossoms filled the air with their fragrance. "Very soon those too will fall to the earth and die," he said. "Just as it is with the blossoms, so it is with you and those you love. Nothing is permanent, so you must not stake your happiness upon things that change. All of life is suffering."

"That is very bleak, Lord," responded a young man in the front of the crowd. He stood close to five of the Buddha's followers, who were also clothed in the yellow-orange robes of a monk. He was a hard-working, optimistic young fellow, apprenticed to an ivory carver. He found this description of life most depressing. "Is there no escape from such suffering?"

The fragrant blossoms of the champaka tree often appear in Buddhist literature.

The Buddha nodded at him encouragingly. "That is why I am here," he replied. "To preach to you the Four Noble Truths so that you too may understand what you must do. It is up to you to listen and to take your lives into your own hands."

The people settled themselves, preparing to hear him explain. Before he could begin, however, another question arose.

"When death takes you from us, Master, will we be able to pray to you for guidance?"

The man who questioned him wore his dark hair in a knot on the right side of his head to indicate that he was a ceremonial Brahmin.[1] He had served his twelve years with a mentor and was now entitled to perform the duties of a priest. His dark eyes regarded the speaker suspiciously as he waited for the answer.

Brahmins were the priests and scholars, a very powerful group.
The teachings of the Buddha removed some of that power from
their hands.

The Buddha shook his head. "I am not a god," he reminded them firmly. "Like others before me, I only point the way for you to follow."

His listeners leaned closer, eager to hear about the path that could lead them from lives of suffering and unhappiness. The young Brahmin, however, kept his distance, remaining at the edge of the crowd.

"Choosing the Middle Way as your path will bring you far more satisfaction than choosing the life of the pleasure-seeking person or the life of the ascetic," the Buddha told them. "Avoid extremes. Do not indulge yourself by satisfying every wish you have, but do not punish yourself by giving up food and proper care for your body so that you cannot think clearly. Instead, live moderately."

He paused for a moment, looking at his listeners. A stranger in the back of the group asked respectfully, "Who are you, Master?"

"We already know who he is," responded another member of the crowd, irritated by yet another interruption. "He is Siddhartha Gautama of the Sakyas."

The others nodded their approval at this mention of a well-known royal clan. It was an honor to have such a person in their midst.

"But you are more than that, are you not?" insisted the stranger, staring intently at the Buddha. "You are more than a mere man, Lord. Are you not indeed a god who has come among us to help us?"

The crowd murmured their approval of this repeated question. Certainly the golden-skinned man before them was most unusual. They were accustomed to having wandering holy men preach to them, but this man was unlike the others. He looked like a king. He spoke with great wisdom and authority. Yet he lived like a very poor man. He treated all people, regardless of their rank, as his equals.

At the time that the Buddha lived, the modern countries of India and Nepal did not exist. Instead, the lands were divided into smaller kingdoms. Throughout these kingdoms, people had grown dissatisfied with the power and secrecy of the Brahmins and their tight control of all formal religious rites. The priests had to be paid—and paid well—to repeat the sacred hymns of the Vedas and to perform the sacrifices that became more and more complicated. Even their language was difficult. The Brahmins used Sanskrit in their rites. This was an ancient language that very few people understood.

Many people had grown weary of such practices. They wondered if they could gain religious knowledge from sources other than the Brahmins. Some had even left their homes to wander from town to town in a quest for truth, searching for the meaning of life and death. Some ascetics lived as hermits deep in the forests, using meditation to search for a deeper knowledge of life. From time to time, a few of these ragged hermits left the forest to share what they had learned there.

Most of the people in the crowd knew that the man before them, Siddhartha Gautama, had given up wealth and power and family in his own quest for truth. Now he lived a life of poverty and spent his time teaching and meditating. He and his followers wandered through the countryside, begging for their meals. Even in a monk's robes, however, he looked less like an ascetic than a prince. Crowds gathered to hear him speak and came to him with their questions and their problems. He spoke quietly and calmly, but with great power and authority. It was little wonder that they had a difficult time deciding just who he really was.

The crowd watched Gautama expectantly, awaiting his reply with eagerness.

The tall man smiled at the people and answered gently. "I am awake," he said simply. For Siddhartha Gautama was a Buddha, and the word "Buddha" means the "Awakened One."[2] A Buddha was one who was enlightened, one who understood the meaning of life and death.

He was not the only Buddha, they knew. There had been Buddhas who lived before Gautama and there would be others who lived after him. However, even today Siddhartha Gautama is still referred to as *the* Buddha. And it was because of Siddhartha Gautama that the religion of Buddhism was born.

The Flowering

Not only the champaka trees flowered during the years that Siddhartha Gautama lived. The Buddha was just one of several extraordinary people who lived during the same period of time in different parts of the world. Their gifts to the rest of mankind were like the scented blossoms of the champaka trees. They offered the comfort of brightness and beauty.

Hundreds of miles to the west, the Greeks were also thinking about the meaning of life and investigating the world around them. Aesop was entertaining his listeners with his fables and their sharp observations about human behavior. These fables, such as the story of the hare and the tortoise, were very much like the parables the Buddha told to illustrate his lessons. A few decades later, Aeschylus and Sophocles started writing the first of the great tragic plays of Greece. Their works marked the beginning of the theater in the Western world. Still another famous Greek was Pythagoras. He was a noted mathematician and philosopher who observed that the earth and the other planets are spheres that move through space.

In Jerusalem, the Jewish prophet Jeremiah was preaching to his people. His speeches and writings were collected into the *Book of Jeremiah*, which would eventually become one of the longest books in the Bible. Several other books of the Old Testament of the Bible were also being written at this time.

In China, Kung Fu-tse (Confucius) was teaching his followers the importance of thinking for themselves and of making ethical decisions in all areas of life, including the government of the country.

Just why all these things happened at this particular time is not clear. It was a time of awakening, questioning, and creating in many parts of the world. The one certain thing is that this era produced a flowering of philosophers whose thoughts still enrich our lives today.

Confucius

13

Before the birth of the Buddha, legends say that his mother, Queen Maya, dreamed of an elephant carrying a lotus flower in its trunk. It touched her side, and she knew that she would have a child.

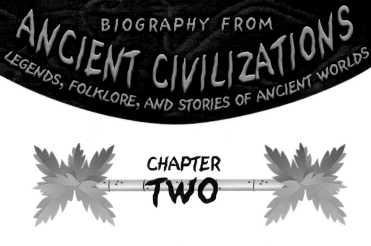
CHAPTER TWO

THE YOUNG PRINCE

Although Siddhartha Gautama was a real person, parts of his life story seem very much like a fairy tale. Indeed, he lived so long ago that many legends have been told about him. Many stories about his life were not written down for centuries. A single story about him may have many variations.

There is even some question about the actual dates of his life. However, most scholars agree that he was born in 563 B.C.E. (Before the Common Era). Historical records kept by the Greeks after Alexander the Great crossed the Indus River (in modern-day Pakistan) have helped to place that date. Those records indicate the year that the Emperor Asoka began his reign. Two separate chronicles from the island of Ceylon (known today as Sri Lanka) indicate that Asoka took the throne 218 years after the death of the Buddha. It is also widely agreed that Buddha lived for 80 years. This information helps to pinpoint the dates of his birth and death.

Some accounts say that Queen Maya, the mother of Siddhartha Gautama, was traveling to visit her parents. It was the custom of the time for women to give birth at their parents' home. But Queen

Maya didn't make it that far. She paused to rest at the garden of Lumbini, the halfway point in her journey. Siddhartha Gautama was born there. Then his mother turned back and went to her home in the town of Kapilavastu. It is located in what is now the country of Nepal. Siddhartha Gautama's father, King Suddhodana, was the town's ruler. The family made preparations for Gautama's name-festival. Unfortunately, Queen Maya died when her son was only a week old. His aunt Pajapati looked after him.

Before the naming of his son, the king invited the family's priest to see the child. After a close inspection, the priest declared that the infant would become a great man. Eight Brahmins who later performed the naming ceremony came to the same conclusion. They said that he would become a "wheel-turner." This is an expression meaning an important man, someone who made things happen or set things in motion. They were certain that his life would command the respect of countless people. They also told the king that Siddhartha Gautama would become either a renowned Buddha or a great king.

King Suddhodana's family belonged to the warrior caste. The king was determined that his son would also become a ruler of men. He did his best to prepare Gautama for that role and to make him contented with his life as a prince. His father was careful to surround him with happy, healthy people. His mother's loss was his only encounter with death.

The boy's life was a very comfortable one. He was handsome and intelligent, and he was given every advantage that wealth and position could offer. He was free to wander in the parks that belonged to the king. He learned the arts of the warrior. He had the company of other young people. Still, he was not always satisfied with his life.

Gautama was given to deep thought, even as a child. He watched the farmers and their oxen in the fields as they strained under a hot sun to plant the crops. He thought about how hard life was for them. He saw how rapidly snow melted away to nothing and how quickly blossoms fell from the trees. He saw that their beauty lasted only a short time. He realized, even then, that all things must change.

When he was sixteen, he married the lovely Princess Yasodhara, whom he loved. Their life together was happy. King Suddhodana was still determined to keep all unpleasant things from his son so he could concentrate on becoming a great ruler. The king did everything possible to keep him connected firmly to the world and satisfied with his life. However, in spite of his lovely wife, his three palaces, and the challenge of learning to be a warrior and a ruler, Gautama was restless.

According to the legends, when he was twenty-nine years old the Four Signs opened his eyes and changed the path of his life.[1]

As the prince rode out one day with his servant, he encountered the First Sign. It was a man at the side of the road. The prince was greatly struck by the man's appearance. His face and body were withered, his eyes were clouded, his mouth was toothless.

"Has he been injured?" Gautama asked his servant in horror. "What is wrong with him?"

"Nothing," replied the servant. "He is merely old."

Gautama shook his head sadly as they rode on. So this was what life held for everyone who managed to grow old. The future looked grim indeed.

As they rode farther, they encountered another man. He was the Second Sign. Although his hair was dark and his figure youthful, he shook like an elderly man and his skin was tinged with gray.

"He is ill, my lord," said the servant when Gautama glanced at him questioningly.

Here was further evidence of the suffering that life could bring. He wondered how long the young man had been ill and if he had ever imagined that he would lose his youth—and probably his life—to disease. Gautama himself had not imagined that such things could happen to anyone, least of all to the young and the strong.

Soon they saw the Third Sign, a man lying beside the road. The prince stopped once again and stared. He did not have to dismount for a closer inspection. The man was undoubtedly dead.

Very depressed, he rode slowly on. What good was being young and happy, he wondered. Illness could destroy health and beauty as quickly as summer sun melts the snow. Death could not be avoided. It came to everyone. No matter how happy someone might be today, such happiness could not, would not, last. Even though he was only twenty-nine years old, he was badly shaken. Life seemed worthless. It was pointless if such suffering and sadness lay ahead of every person.

Sunk as he was in depression, Gautama did not at first see the monk walking toward him along the road. Finally he noticed the man's bright saffron robe and shaven head.

As Gautama reached the monk's side, he slowed his horse's pace. He was greatly impressed by the man's contented expression.

"Who are you?" he asked the monk.

"A seeker of truth," was the reply. "I am searching for freedom from pain and death."

"And do you think you will find it?" asked Gautama eagerly. "Is it possible?" For a moment he felt hope ripple over him. Perhaps there was a way to avoid the pain and unhappiness that he had witnessed that day and help others to do so.

"I can but try," said the monk. "It is for that I live."

He bowed his head to the prince and continued on his way. The monk was the Fourth Sign.

Very slowly Gautama rode back to his palace, knowing that it would be for the last time. His decision was made. The Four Signs had convinced him. He too would become a seeker of truth. He too would look for the answer of life over death. Somehow he had to find a way to make sense of the things that he had seen. He could not think of any other worthwhile purpose for his life.

Some of the stories say that his wife gave birth to their first child, a boy, on that very night. Gautama named him Rahula, which means "chain." He saw the boy as yet another tie to his life in the palace. In spite of his love for his family, he was determined to free himself from them so that he could begin his quest. He knew that his work would take the rest of his life. He would have no time to spare for his family or for becoming a ruler of men.

Later that night, he cut off his hair and rode away from his old life. He left a message for his family, telling them not to grieve for him. Death would have separated them sooner or later.[2]

As he rode once more down the road, he again encountered the monk. The man appeared silently from the forest, handing Gautama a saffron robe of his own and a begging bowl.

After many years, the Buddha once more visited Kapilavastu, attended by his followers.

Siddhartha Gautama was no longer a prince with a life of privilege. He set forth on his quest to find the answer of life over death.

Whether or not things happened in just this manner is, of course, not certain. However, the story of the four encounters has become an enduring part of Siddhartha Gautama's story. It offers an explanation of the reason he chose to leave his family and a life of luxury for the difficult and lonely path he had to follow to become a Buddha.

Ancient Medicine

Medical schools existed during the time that the Buddha lived, even though they were very different from modern institutions that train men and women to become doctors. At that time, students simply studied with their teachers. The medicine they learned was called *Ayurveda*, which means "knowledge of life."

A surgeon named Sushruta and a physician named Charaka recorded much of what was known about the early practice of *Ayurveda* in two ancient collections, the *Sushruta Samhita* and the *Charaka Samhita*. Although the exact dates of those two doctors' lives are not known, the Greek conqueror Alexander the Great found that the practice of medicine was already very advanced when he invaded India in 326 B.C.E.

From approximately 800 B.C.E. to 1000 C.E., the Brahmins were in charge of Indian medicine because they were the priests and scholars. During that period, the city of Benares was an important center for medical study. Numerous hospitals also existed in India during these early times. According to an inscription in stone recorded in 226 B.C.E., the Emperor Asoka was responsible for building several hospitals.

Even though we often think of all early medicine as primitive, the Indian surgeons of the time performed several very difficult procedures. Since people were often injured in battle or were punished by the amputation of a nose or an ear, surgeons learned how to reconstruct the missing nose or ear. Astonishingly, they used some of the same techniques in skin grafting that are used by plastic surgeons today. They were also able to perform intestinal surgery and to operate for cataracts, a clouding of the lens of the eye. Sushruta himself was credited with the first cataract operation.

The practice of medicine included much more than surgery, however. Physicians encouraged proper diet and exercise, as well as the practice of good hygiene. Ancient medical writings also include descriptions of a great number of diseases and specific suggestions for their treatment.

FYI

For Your Info

Dr. Mangas Ayurveda,
Wellness & Yoga Zentrum

AYURVEDA

AYURVEDA:
SCHENKT DIR GESUNDHEIT VITALITÄT
SCHÖNHEIT UND HARMONIE

*Know and feel
the hands of healing*

The Buddha is often associated with the lotus position, a yoga position used for meditation. This position allows the individual to sit for long periods of time without movement.

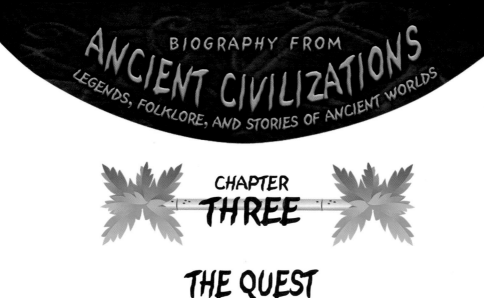
CHAPTER
THREE

THE QUEST

After leaving his old life behind him, Gautama made his way to two Hindu masters to study with them. He hoped he would learn how to end suffering for himself and others from these two gurus.

With them, he would have studied the *Upanishads.*[1] These are a set of ancient Hindu scriptures. The concepts of rebirth and karma were very important in these teachings. According to these beliefs, after death a person's soul is reborn in another body. It could be a human, an animal, or even an insect.[2] The form is determined by an individual's karma, the accumulation of things the person has said and done during the course of all earlier lives. If the karma is good—that is, if the person has behaved in a worthy manner—at death the person will be reborn into a better life. If the karma is bad, the new life will provide the punishment for those past actions and words. The soul goes on in an endless cycle of rebirths. These teachings would have greatly influenced Gautama's thinking.

Another important teaching was that the individual soul is the essence, or real self, of a person. In the same way, the universe itself and everything within it has an essence. Many believed that the individual soul and the universal soul are one and the same. At the time that Gautama lived, some had come to believe that having the soul of the individual reunite with the universal soul could end the cycle of death and rebirth.[3]

Gautama also undoubtedly studied yoga with the Hindu masters. He would have learned to discipline his body through the postures of yoga. Through the control of body posture and breathing, the mind becomes disciplined and focused for meditation. The individual is then prepared to learn knowledge of the self. One of the most famous yoga postures is the Padmasana, better known as the "lotus position." The individual sits cross-legged, with the soles of the feet and the palms of the hands turned upwards. This position is still associated with the Buddha today. Many statues show him in the lotus position.

Gautama learned as much as he could from the two masters. He could see that it would not be enough to answer his questions. He could not complete his quest with the gurus. He had learned much, but he did not see how to find an end to suffering. He set forth once more.

He next joined five ascetics with whom he spent several years. In their search for understanding, the ascetics were very strict. They starved themselves and denied themselves physical comforts. Gautama adopted their methods. He hoped that doing so would help him find the answer for which he searched. Perhaps, he thought, severe discipline of his body would improve his mind's ability to see the truth.

For a long time he allowed himself only a few drops of soup each day. He was so thin that he could feel his backbone when he placed his hand on his stomach. He was close to death. He survived only because a young girl passing by with her herd of cows took pity on him. She stopped and fed him a bowl of rice gruel.

As his strength returned, he realized that starving himself had not helped to clear his mind. He remembered a time from his youth when he had sat under a rose-apple tree, watching a farmer plow the field with his oxen. At the time, everything had suddenly seemed very clear to him. For a moment he had clearly seen the world as it was. This memory convinced him that understanding would not come to him more easily because he deprived himself of food.

He was certain now that the ascetics could not help him in his quest. The truth could not be found through either a life of indulgence or a life of self-denial. He decided that the seeker of truth needed to choose the Middle Way between the two.

When he told the ascetics of his decision, they were disgusted and left him. They considered him a weakling. He was not strong enough to deny himself the temptations of life—such as a bowl of rice gruel.

Gautama was not bothered by their attitude. He felt that he was very close to finding the answer to his question. Finally, on a pleasant night in May, he seated himself under a fig tree. It became known as the Bo (or Bodhi) Tree. Gautama swore that he would not move from that place until he had found the answer to his question. The place where he sat was later named the Immovable Spot.

Gautama was not the only one who suspected he was nearing the end of his quest. According to Buddhist scriptures, an evil god named Mara tried to tempt him. Mara wanted to frighten him away so that he could not achieve enlightenment and find the answers he sought. Gautama would not allow himself to be distracted. He stayed firmly in his place under the tree and entered a state of meditation, ignoring Mara.

In the first watch of the night,[4] Gautama relived all of his past lives. They numbered in the thousands. He saw clearly how his actions—good and evil—had affected his development and had finally brought him to the Bo Tree that night. He saw the law of karma, of cause and effect, at work in his own lives. In the second watch of the night, he saw all the living creatures in the universe. Karma was at work in their lives as well.

In the third watch he had his moment of enlightenment and completed his quest. Suddenly he saw life as it was. He understood how everything fit together. He saw the interplay of cause and effect among all the living creatures in the universe. He saw that the actions of the individual creature affected not only its existence but that of countless others as well.

When he reached his understanding, Gautama discovered at last how to free himself and others from suffering, from the cycle of death and rebirth. According to the legends, flowers showered down upon him like snowflakes. The earth quaked in honor of his achievement. Gautama—now the Buddha—remained under the tree for 49 days, lost in happiness.

It is said that Mara tried one last time to tempt him. This time he urged the Buddha not to share what he had learned. He said that others would not be able to understand it. The Buddha paused. It was tempting to consider keeping the happy knowledge to himself instead of returning to the world to share it with others. He thought about it. Then he shook his head. He said that some people would understand him. That was enough. He denied himself a comfortable existence and chose instead to help others. With that act of self-sacrifice, Mara was finally banished. The Buddha was ready to teach others what he had learned.[5]

The Jataka Tales

From a *Jataka Tale*

The *Jataka Tales* are the stories of the Buddha's previous lives before he became Siddhartha Gautama. During those earlier lives, he was a "bodhisattva" or a "Buddha-in-training." All of these lives prepared him for becoming a Buddha.

About 550 of those stories have survived, and they have been used for a variety of purposes. Many show specific lessons that helped him along the road to Buddhahood. In some of them he even meets other Buddhas who recognize his promise and encourage him to continue his efforts to reach that state himself.

Other stories show his connection in earlier lives to people who were important to him during his final life as Gautama, such as his mother and his wife and some of his followers. Occasionally the stories reveal the reasons for current problems in relationships, problems that had their roots in earlier lives. Some of the stories also serve to show that the Buddha was not always perfect.

It is not uncommon for him to appear as an animal in the *Jataka Tales*. In one, for instance, he is a stag, and he gives his life to save his herd. In another, he is a rabbit that throws himself into a fire in order to save a Brahmin who is starving. Self-sacrifice is a frequent theme for the stories.

As Buddhism spread to other lands, the *Jataka Tales* absorbed some of the heroes and folk tales of those places, giving the Buddha and the religion of Buddhism connections in those countries. Many of the animal tales are told in the same form as Aesop's fables, often with similar characters and morals. The Buddha used them as parables to teach lessons to his followers. In fact, the animal tales in particular are much like other stories told in India, as well as China and surrounding countries. Which stories were told first or whether they sprang up at the same time as people began to be interested in teaching lessons about moral behavior is still a matter for debate.

The Golden Buddha of Thailand, made of pure gold, is 15'9" high and weighs approximately 5 tons. It is more than 700 years old, but it was "discovered" only in the 1950s. Long ago it had been covered with plaster so that it would not be stolen, and only when the plaster covering was accidentally broken in 1955 was the Golden Buddha rediscovered.

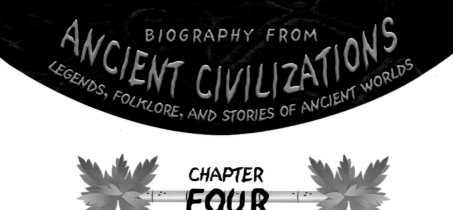
CHAPTER
FOUR

THE WHEEL-TURNER

After his experience under the Bo Tree, the Buddha made a long journey to the town of Sarnath. At the Deer Park there, he found the five ascetics with whom he had lived for so long. He preached his first sermon to them. It has been called "Setting in Motion the Wheel of Dharma" and "The Turning of the Wheel." Considering the prediction of the priests at his birth, the title was appropriate. At thirty-five years of age he had at last become a "wheel-turner." The sermon taught his listeners how to live in harmony with the way things are in the universe. With it, he set a wheel in motion. It still is turning 2,500 years later.

At first the ascetics were still upset with him. He had left them for what they considered a wasteful life of luxury. They did not want to listen to him. They were, in fact, inclined to ignore him when he told them that he was now a Buddha. Finally they agreed to pay attention to him. His discovery had given him an air of authority. They seated themselves and were the first to hear of the Four Noble Truths and the Eightfold Path in his sermon.

Once the Buddha had seen the universe as it truly is, he approached the problem that he saw there in a very orderly, logical manner. In fact, he approached it in the same manner that a doctor would have diagnosed a patient who was ill. The first step was to observe the patient's illness, the second to determine the cause of the illness, the third to decide whether the cause could be eliminated, and the fourth to prescribe the treatment that would cure the illness.

Using that pattern, he identified the Four Noble Truths,[1] and he presented them to his listeners.

1. Life is filled with suffering. Sometimes people are unhappy for obvious reasons. They may be chained to jobs or situations that they dislike. Even when people are happy, they are fearful of disease and death, of losing the people or the things they love. Neither happiness nor life itself is permanent. Therefore, suffering is always present, even if it is disguised for the moment by happiness.

2. The cause of suffering is desire. Here the Buddha referred to the desire of individuals to have their own wishes granted. They concentrate on themselves instead of seeing themselves as a part of the whole (the universal soul to which he felt all creatures belong). When people focus on themselves as separate units and are trapped by trying to satisfy their own selfish needs, suffering follows.

3. Suffering stops when desire stops. By this, however, the Buddha did not mean that suffering stops only with death. Here he referred again to selfish desires that focused only on individual needs. He encouraged desiring happiness for others and working for the good of others.

4. The way to end selfish desires is to follow the Eightfold Path.

The Buddha then proceeded to lay out the Eightfold Path in the same logical, precise manner that he had used to identify the Four Noble Truths. The Eightfold Path is his "prescription" for putting an end to suffering. It is therefore tightly linked to the Four Noble Truths.

1. Right Understanding. In order to start down the Eightfold Path, people must understand the Four Noble Truths and the reason for choosing this course of action.

2. Right Intentions. People must be firmly convinced that following the Eightfold Path is what they wish to do.

The next three steps taken along the Path require people to take specific actions in their lives. These are acts that require self-discipline and that affect daily behavior.

3. Right Speech. The followers of the Eightfold Path need to consider their words carefully. What they say will not be free from fault, but they should aim for truthfulness and kindness.

4. Right Action. They should think about the motives for their actions. Actions should be caused by selflessness and kindness, not selfishness or cruelty. Also, they are not to kill, to lie, to steal, to engage in sexual misconduct, or to take intoxicants. All their actions should show respect for others.

5. Right Livelihood. Followers of the Path should earn their living in ways that show respect for all living creatures and allow them to continue their own moral and spiritual growth. The Buddha identified specific occupations that should be avoided, such as being a slave trader.

The last three steps of the Path also require self-discipline. This time, however, it is the mind that must be disciplined.

6. Right Effort. Reaching the final goal requires steady effort. Although the Buddha saw clearly the workings of cause and effect in karma, he believed that people must work to improve themselves and their situations.

It was under the Bodhi Tree that Siddhartha Gautama reached his enlightenment and became the "Awakened One."

7. Right Mindfulness. This step requires that people become very aware (or "mindful") of their own minds and bodies. They should notice when moods and feelings change, not because they want to judge those moods and feelings as good or bad, but just for the sake of noticing what they are and how rapidly they change.

8. Right Concentration. In this step, people must focus their minds and meditate. In this way, like the Buddha, they may also see things as they really are.

When Siddhartha Gautama had reached his time of understanding under the Bodhi Tree and became the Buddha, he had attained living nirvana. This is the state of great happiness in which he was free from all desires. He could have chosen, as some others had, to become a Buddha-for-himself-alone, keeping all of his knowledge to himself. Some accounts say that he could have chosen to leave his body then and enter a state of nirvana immediately. However, he decided to return to the world to share what he had learned with others.

The five ascetics listened carefully to his sermon. They joyfully attained enlightenment and became his followers. The Buddha began a period of 45 years of preaching the Dharma. Other people besides the ascetics wished to follow him. He soon established a community of religious followers called the sangha. The Buddha was invited to visit King Bimbisara, the ruler of Magadha. The king was so impressed by the Buddha's teaching that he gave him a pleasure park beyond the town as a retreat. That bamboo grove became the Buddha's first permanent monastic park.

When the Buddha's father, King Suddhodana, heard that his son was traveling nearby, he sent a messenger asking him to come and visit his family. The Buddha and his followers stayed in a park at the edge of town and begged for their meals. Many people from Kapilavastu came to hear his teachings. Some became his followers. They included several members of his family—his wife Yasodhara, his son Rahula, and his aunt Pajapati, who had helped to raise him. Pajapati also established the first community of Buddhist nuns. Ananda, one of his cousins, became his chief disciple and served him for the remainder of the Buddha's life.

Death came to the Buddha at the age of 80, when he accepted a meal from a blacksmith named Cunda. According to some stories, the Buddha knew that the meat he was offered was spoiled. He ate it rather than hurt Cunda's feelings. When he realized that he was dying, he made his way to the village of Kushinagara and lay down in a grove of trees there. Even in death, he remembered to send a message to Cunda. He told Cunda not to be distressed. The meal was releasing him from the cycle of death and rebirth. Now he was entering the joyful state of completed nirvana.

The eight-spoked Wheel of Dharma is a symbol of Buddhist Law and its Eightfold Path. Such wheels were common even before the time of Emperor Asoka.

Nor would he allow his followers to be sorrowful. He told them that his death was a time for rejoicing. He had reached his goal. He asked them if they had any questions. No one did. Nor was anyone appointed to take his place. Instead, he said, they would have to rely upon the Dharma. At the moment of his death, like the moment of his enlightenment, it is said that flower petals fell over him like snowflakes.[2]

The Buddha had many achievements. He founded an order of Buddhist monks that still exists today. In a time when such an action was extraordinary, he allowed women to be a part of the religious community. Nor did he recognize caste. He spoke with kings and beggars and treated them equally. Unlike the Brahmin priests, he presented his teachings to the people in their own language rather than the ancient Sanskrit that few could understand. He kept no secrets from people, sharing with them everything he knew and understood.

He had set the Wheel of Dharma in motion with his first sermon 45 years earlier. It is still turning today, 2,500 years later.

Places of Pilgrimage

Although there are many places that are sacred to the memory of the Buddha, four are particularly special. People have been visiting these sites since the time of the Buddha's death.

One is Lumbini, Nepal, which is believed to have been his birthplace. In 249 B.C.E., the Emperor Asoka visited the garden and had a stone pillar erected there in honor of the Buddha. The Maya Devi temple, which was built in honor of his mother, is also located there. Not far from Lumbini is the site where Kapilavastu, the home of his childhood and youth, was once located. The earliest of the ruins there date back to the eighth century B.C.E.

Maha Bodhi Temple

Another site that many visit is Bodh Gaya, the place of the Buddha's enlightenment and his Immovable Spot. The Emperor Asoka also visited there, and it is said that he ordered the temple of Maha Bodhi to be built there. The original Bodhi Tree is not still there, of course. According to tradition, the present tree, which grows close to the temple, is one of its descendants. Tradition also states that the emperor's daughter, who went to Ceylon as a Buddhist nun, took a shoot from the original tree with her. She planted it at a monastery there, where it can still be found.

The Deer Park at Sarnath, where he delivered his first sermon, is also a place that many pilgrims visit. A stupa said to have been erected by Emperor Asoka still remains among the extensive ruins.

The place of his death, the village of Kushinagara, has a 1500-year-old statue of the Buddha carved from a single piece of red sandstone. A British officer made camp here during the 1800s and investigated the temple mound, which had been covered over by jungle growth. He unearthed the statue, which was badly broken, and managed to find enough of the pieces to repair it. As a result, Kushinagara, the site of the Buddha's completed nirvana, is once again a destination for pilgrims.

Vajrayana Buddhism is prevalent in the countries of the Himalayas. Vajrasattva, a Buddha remaining in a Bodhisattva (Buddha-in-training) form so that he could help others to enlightenment, is an important figure in this school of Buddhism.

CHAPTER
FIVE

AFTER THE BUDDHA

At the time when Buddha died, he left more than 500 monks behind him to share the Dharma with others. Three months later, these monks met to collect his teachings. Once they had agreed on these teachings, the monks committed them to memory. Succeeding generations of monks repeated them carefully for hundreds of years before they were finally recorded.

It was not until about 83 B.C.E. in Ceylon that the Buddhist scriptures were first written down on palm leaves. Some of the monks felt that it was important to have a permanent record in writing. Differences were beginning to appear in the oral versions. The scriptures were written in the Pali language. They were called the Tipitaka, which means "three baskets." The scriptures were divided into three groups. Each group was stored in a separate basket, so there actually were three baskets. One held writings about the sangha, the community of monks and nuns. A second held the sermons and stories of the Buddha. The third held writings that commented about the teachings of Buddhism.[1]

Differences in belief had also arisen among the Buddhists at about the same time. The religion splintered into several groups.

Theravada Buddha statues are simple. The Buddha wears a plain robe, and the lines of the statue are smooth. It is a symbol for the principles that the Buddha taught.

The two major groups were known as Theravada Buddhism and Mahayana Buddhism. There are numerous differences between them. Theravadin Buddhists believe that individuals reach nirvana by their own efforts. They consider the Buddha a great teacher and a saint but not a god. Mahayanists, on the other hand, believe that Buddhahood is reached with divine help. They consider the Buddha a savior.

The Theravadins used the Tipitaka as the basis for their studies. About 200 years after it was recorded, the Mahayanists met to record their own version of the scriptures. They called it the Tripitaka, which means "three baskets" in Sanskrit. It is divided into the same categories and has primarily the same writings, although it does contain some extra pieces.

Over the first few centuries of the Common Era, Buddhism spread across Southeast Asia to Burma, Thailand, Laos, and Cambodia. To the north it spread into Tibet, China, Vietnam, Korea, and Japan. Theravada Buddhism (also called the School of the Elders because it considered itself closest to the teachings of the Buddha) spread to the south and Mahayana Buddhism (known as the Great Vehicle because it felt it had the power to carry many people—not just monks and nuns—to enlightenment) to the north. By the fifth century C.E., Vajrayana Buddhism (known as the Diamond Way) had appeared in India. It is a form of Mahayana Buddhism, but it also includes the use of tantras (guidebooks) that explain such things as the use of magic rituals and complicated yoga practices. This form of Buddhism also made its way to Nepal, Tibet, and Japan.

In each country, the religion adapted to the particular needs of that people, changing somewhat in form as Zen Buddhism has done in Japan. Buddhism has always had the power to blend with different cultures to serve the needs of the people. The beliefs stated in the Eightfold Path have served to strengthen and improve governmental leaders as well as the people they rule.

As the number of Buddhists was growing in other countries, however, by about 1000 C.E. Buddhism seems to have virtually vanished as a religion from India. Hinduism absorbed all of Buddhism's main teachings, treating it as a sort of reformation of the early Hindu religion rather than a separate religion. In spite of this rather strange situation, Buddhism is still a force to be reckoned with in India. The spoked wheel that is a symbol of the Dharma stands at the center of the country's flag.[2]

More recently, Buddhism made its way to Europe and North America. The California gold rush of 1849 attracted many Chinese immigrants to that state. By 1870 their number had increased to more than 60,000. Many brought their Buddhist traditions and faith. So have other Asian immigrants during the past century. During the past fifty years, a number of Americans who are from a less traditional background have become interested in Buddhism.

Vesak is a joyful celebration in honor of the Buddha's birth, his enlightenment, and death. Gifts of food and flowers are taken to the monasteries, and people do good deeds for others, just as the Buddha would have wished. Incense is burned in his honor, flowers are brought to shrines, and people carry candles and lanterns that night to symbolize that the Buddha was a light to others.

During the past century, Buddhists in some Asian lands—such as Cambodia, Tibet, China, and Mongolia—have suffered because of oppressive governments. In Cambodia between 1975 and 1979, for instance, it is estimated that more than 60,000 monks were killed. In Mongolia, more than 20,000 monks were killed during the 1930s when the practice of any religion was banned under the communist government. In 1990, religious freedom was allowed once more. Since then, temples and monasteries have been restored and Buddhist schools reestablished. Once again Buddhism is showing signs of flourishing in places where its growth was controlled or banned.[3]

The Buddha has been dead for almost 2,500 years, but he is far from forgotten. Vesak is a holiday celebrated by Buddhists around the globe. The birth, enlightenment, and death of the Buddha are celebrated during the full moon in May. People who know nothing

The lotus has long been associated with the Buddha. Growing from a seed deep in the darkness, it reaches for the light, symbolizing the desire for enlightenment. According to legend, it appeared in the Buddha's life even before he was born, when his mother dreamed of the elephant carrying a lotus blossom in its trunk. And no doubt lotus blossoms were among those that showered down upon him at his enlightenment and at his death.

about Buddha recognize him in pictures and statues. They know he was renowned for his wisdom.

One of the best-known symbols of the Buddha and his teaching is the lotus, whose unfolding blossoms represent the unfolding of the human understanding as it moves toward enlightenment. Just as the lotus grows from the mud and rises above the water to bloom, the person who follows the Eightfold Path rises above worldly concerns toward the promise of nirvana.

Long ago the Buddha refused complete nirvana for himself. He turned back to the world, where he devoted 45 years to teaching the Dharma to countless followers. Millions more have read his words over the centuries. His self-sacrifice remains both an example and a challenge to those who have followed him.

FYI
For Your Info

The Emperor Asoka

Two hundred years after his death, Buddha gained an impressive new follower—the Emperor Asoka, ruler of the Mauryan Empire. He was a mighty ruler whose empire included northern India and Pakistan.

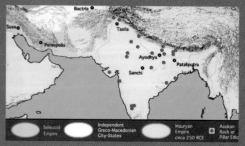

Map of Mauryan Empire

Asoka was probably born around 300 B.C.E. and became emperor when he was in his mid-30s. Several years later he began a war against a neighboring kingdom. Heartsick after a bloody campaign that had cost more than 100,000 lives, he became a Buddhist and changed his manner of life. He gave up war and even hunting, and conducted himself during the rest of his reign in a manner that the Buddha would have approved.

He did his best for his people. He ruled wisely, building hospitals, planting banyan trees and groves of mangoes along the roadsides, erecting places for travelers to rest, supporting Buddhist monasteries, and recommending kind treatment of all living creatures. In spite of his deep belief in Buddhism, he was tolerant of other religions.

He visited the sites associated with the Buddha's life and erected many stupas in Buddha's honor. For instance, the Bodhi tree where the Buddha first became enlightened was enclosed by a stone fence and marked as a sacred place with a pillar. The emperor sent a shoot of the tree to the ruler of Ceylon. Asoka also sponsored a council of Buddhist leaders and sent Buddhist missionaries to many different lands. It is said that he sent his own son, a Buddhist monk, and his daughter, a Buddhist nun, to Ceylon. The emperor even sent missionaries as far away as Greece and Egypt to share the Buddha's teachings with the world. He did his best to spread Buddhism to the far corners of the world.

Scholars aren't sure exactly when he died, though the best estimates are between 239 and 233 B.C.E. His empire didn't last much longer. Some historians believe that the peaceful ways he emphasized were responsible for its downfall.

Chronology

(All dates Before Common Era)*

563	Born in May in the garden at Lumbini, in modern-day Nepal
547	Marries Princess Yasodhara
534	Becomes father when son Rahula is born
534	Leaves Kapilavastu on his quest for enlightenment
528	Achieves enlightenment as he sits under the Bodhi Tree
528	Preaches his first sermon, "The Turning of the Wheel"
483	Dies at the village of Kushinagara

*Please note that dates are approximate

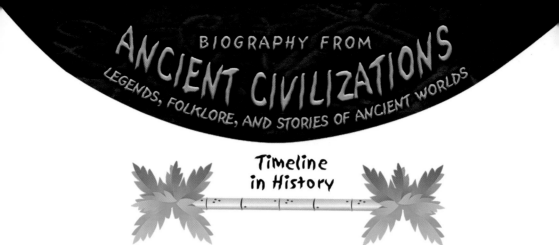

Timeline in History

(All dates Before Common Era)*

1100–500	The Vedas, sacred literature of the Hindus, are recorded during this period.
604	The Chinese philosopher Lao-tse is born.
599	Mahavira, a Jain prophet and the first to rebel against the caste system in India, is born.
581	Pythagoras, Greek mathematician and philosopher, is born.
553	Cyrus the Great begins his reign and makes Persia a great empire.
551	Philosopher K'ung Fu-tzu (Confucius) is born in China.
536	Milo of Crotona wins the first of his five successive wrestling championships at the Olympic Games.
525	Bimbisara begins his reign as King of Magadha, a kingdom in eastern India.
524	The Greek dramatist Aeschylus is born.
517	Darius, king of Persia, sends an expedition to explore the Indus River.
509	The Romans drive out their king and declare a republic.
500	Sushrata, one of the most famous surgeons in ancient India, begins performing cataract operations.
500–450	Dams are constructed in India.
490	A messenger runs miles from Marathon to Athens to announce that the Greeks had defeated an invading Persian army. This run becomes the basis of the modern marathon race.
484	The Greek historian Herodotus, known as the Father of History, is born.
483	The 500 monks who have followed the Buddha meet after his death to collect his teachings.
470	The Greek philosopher Socrates is born in Athens.
460	Hippocrates, a Greek who is often referred to as the "Father of Medicine," is born.
431	The Temple of Apollo is built in Rome.

*Please note that some dates are approximate

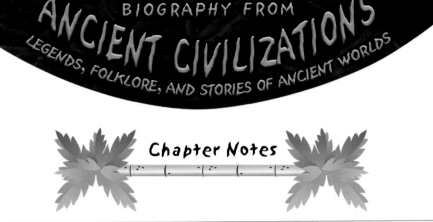

Chapter Notes

CHAPTER ONE   THE BUDDHA

The dialogue in this and other chapters represents the author's interpretation of what might have happened, based on her extensive research, and is solely an aid to readability.

1. Brahmins were members of the priestly caste. In the Buddha's time, the people were divided into four groups, or castes: the priestly caste, the warrior caste, the merchant and farmer caste, and the servant caste. The Brahmins were generally considered the most powerful group.

2. Huston Smith and Philip Novak, *Buddhism* (New York: HarperCollins Publishers, Inc., 2003), p. 4.

CHAPTER TWO   THE YOUNG PRINCE

1. John S. Strong, *The Buddha: A Short Biography* (Oxford, United Kingdom: Oneworld Publications, 2001), p. 47.

2. Huston Smith and Philip Novak, *Buddhism* (New York: HarperCollins Publishers, Inc., 2003), p. 7.

CHAPTER THREE   THE QUEST

1. These teachings were composed over a period of several hundred years (800–450 B.C.E.), including the time that the Buddha lived. They dealt with the relationship of an individual to the universe and were often written in dialogue form.

2. This rebirth of the soul is sometimes referred to as reincarnation or the transmigration of the soul.

3. Madhu Bazaz Wangu, *Hinduism. World Religions* (New York: Facts on File, 2002), p. 36.

4. In ancient times, the night was divided into "watches." The first watch was from dusk until 10 PM, the second from 10 PM until 2 AM, and the third from 2 AM until dawn.

5. Huston Smith and Philip Novak, *Buddhism* (New York: HarperCollins Publishers, Inc., 2003), p. 12.

CHAPTER FOUR   THE WHEEL-TURNER

1. Huston Smith and Philip Novak, *Buddhism* (New York: HarperCollins Publishers, Inc., 2003), p. 32.

2. John S. Strong, *The Buddha: A Short Biography* (Oxford, United Kingdom: Oneworld Publications, 2001), p. 137.

CHAPTER FIVE   AFTER THE BUDDHA

1. Madhu Bazaz Wangu, *World Religions: Buddhism* (New York: Facts on File, 2002), p. 70.

2. Huston Smith and Philip Novak, *Buddhism* (New York: HarperCollins Publishers, Inc., 2003), p. 118.

3. Wangu, p. 113.

Glossary

ascetic	(uh-SEH-tick)—one who lives a life of great self-denial.
B.C.E.	—Before the Common Era.
bodhisattva	(bow-dih-SOT-vuh)—a future Buddha.
C.E.	—Common Era.
dharma	(DAR-muh)—the teachings of the Buddha.
enlightenment	(in-LIE-ten-ment)—the state of understanding the truth; being freed from desire and suffering.
guru	(GOO-roo)—a spiritual master or guide.
Hindu	(HIN-doo)—a follower of Hinduism.
karma	(CAR-muh)—the sum of a person's past lives that determines his or her fate in the next life.
meditation	(meh-duh-TAY-shun)—deep, continued thought, often about a sacred subject.
monk	(munk)—a man belonging to a religious order and living by its rules.
nirvana	(nir-VAH-nuh)—the happy state of being free from the endless cycle of death and rebirth.
nun	(NONE)—a woman belonging to a religious order and living by its rules.
pilgrimage	(PILL-gruh-mij)—a journey to a shrine or holy place.
rites	(RIGHTS)—ceremonial actions that follow a carefully defined pattern, often of a religious nature.
saffron	(SA-frun)—orangish yellow color of monks' robes.
samsara	(sum-SAHR-uh)—the endless cycle of death and rebirth.
sangha	(SUNG-guh)—a Buddhist religious community.
stupa	(STOO-puh)— a dome-like mound marking a Buddhist shrine.
Vedas	(VAY-duz)—four collections of sacred Hindu literature.

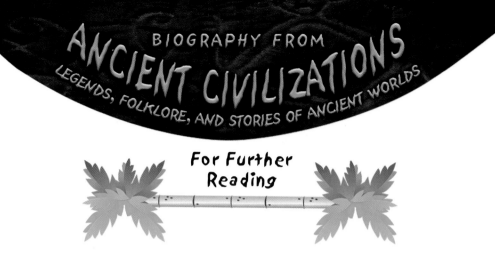
For Further Reading

For Young Adults

Chödzin, Sherab and Alexandra Kohn. *The Wisdom of the Crows and Other Buddhist Tales*. Berkeley, CA: Tricycle Press, 1998.

Demi. *Buddha*. New York: Henry Holt and Company, Inc., 1996.

———. *Buddha Stories*. New York: Henry Holt and Company, Inc., 1997.

Hewitt, Catherine. *Buddhism*. New York: Thomson Learning, 1995.

Marchant, Kerena. *The Buddha and Buddhism*. North Mankato, MN: Smart Apple Media, 2003.

Works Consulted

Daniélon, Alain. *A Brief History of India*. Rochester, VT: Inner Traditions International, 2003.

Dolan, John P., and William N. Adams-Smith. *Health and Society: A Documentary History of Medicine*. New York: The Seabury Press, 1978.

Porter, Roy. *The Greatest Benefit to Mankind*. New York: W. W. Norton & Company, 1997.

Schumann, H. W. *The Historical Buddha*. Translated by M. O'C. Walshe. London, England: Arkana, 1989.

Schulberg, Lucille and the editors of *Time-Life Books*. Historic India. *Great Ages of Man: A History of the World's Cultures*. New York: Time-Life Books, 1968.

Smith, Huston and Philip Novak. *Buddhism*. New York: HarperCollins Publishers, Inc., 2003.

Strong, John S. *The Buddha: A Short Biography*. Oxford, England: Oneworld Publications. 2001.

Wangu, Madhu Bazaz. *World Religions: Buddhism*. New York: Facts on File, Inc., 2002.

———. *World Religions: Hinduism*. New York: Facts on File, Inc., 1991.

Woods, Michael and Mary B. Woods. *Ancient Medicine: From Sorcery to Surgery*. Minneapolis, MN: Runestone Press, 2000.

On the Internet

About Kushinagar
http://www.kushinagar.com

Buddhist Sites In India
http://www.ebudhaindia.com

Introduction to Buddhism
http://buddhanet.net/e-learning/intro_bud.htm

Yoga Asanas: Padmasana
http://www.kevala.co.uk/yoga/asana2.cfm

Index